Countries Around the World
Libya

Nick Hunter

www.raintreepublishers.co.uk

Visit our website to find out more information about Raintree books.

To order:

☎ Phone 0845 6044371
🖹 Fax +44 (0) 1865 312263
🖳 Email myorders@raintreepublishers.co.uk

Customers from outside the UK please telephone +44 1865 312262

Raintree is an imprint of Capstone Global Library Limited, a company incorporated in England and Wales having its registered office at 7 Pilgrim Street, London, EC4V 6LB – Registered company number: 6695582

Edited by Abby Colich and Megan Cotugno
Designed by Philippa Jenkins
Original illustrations © Capstone Global Library Ltd.
Illustrated by Oxford Designers & Illustrators
Picture research by Liz Alexander
Originated by Capstone Global Library Ltd.
Printed in China by CTPS

ISBN 978 1 406 23564 7 (hardback)
16 15 14 13 12
10 9 8 7 6 5 4 3 2 1

British Library Cataloguing in Publication Data
Hunter, Nick.

Libya. -- (Countries around the world)

1. Libya--Juvenile literature.

I. Title II. Series

961.2'042-dc22

Acknowledgments
We would like to thank the following for permission to reproduce photographs: Alamy: pp. 21 (© Oliver Gerhard), 22 (© Charles O. Cecil), 27 (© Paul Doyle), 29 (© John Warburton-Lee Photography), 32 (© MARKA); Capstone Global Library, Ltd: p. 33 (Philippa Jenkins); Corbis: p. 25 (© John Van Hasselt); Dreamstime. com: p. 20 (© Igorj); Getty Images: pp. 8 (Rolls Press/Popperfoto), 15 (Reza), 17 (Benjamin Lowy), 19 (Bashar Shglila), 23 (Philippe Bourseiller), 31 (Reza), 34 (Marwan Naamani/AFP), 35 (Benjamin Lowy); iStockphoto: p. 13 (© AmandaLewis); Photolibrary: p. 30 (JTB Photo); Shutterstock: pp. 5 (© Pascal Rateau), 6 (© Pascal Rateau), 7 (© John Copland), 9 (© Pascal Rateau), 10 (© Mark III Photonics), 28 (© apdesign), 39 (© Styve Reineck), 46 (© Route66).

Cover photograph of gates leading to the centre of the old medina, Tripoli, Libya, reproduced with permission from Photolibrary (Ken Scicluna).

We would like to thank Shiera S. el-Malik for her invaluable help in the preparation of this book.

Every effort has been made to contact copyright holders of material reproduced in this book. Any omissions will be rectified in subsequent printings if notice is given to the publisher.

Contents

Some words are printed in bold, **like this**. You can find out what they mean by looking in the glossary.

Introducing Libya

Libya is a country of contrasts. Most of the North African country's people live in major cities along the long Mediterranean coast, but the Sahara Desert, which covers much of North Africa, dominates this vast and ancient country.

Ancient and modern

Libya's **economy** is largely based on its huge reserves of oil beneath the desert sands. The oil industry has made Libya a wealthy country. However, outside the main cities, many Libyan people raise animals the way they were raised centuries ago.

Despite the unchanging way of life for many of its people, Libya is a very modern country. Wealth from oil has helped to provide health care and education. The culture of Libya is based on traditional family and tribal groups – and strict following of **Islam**.

Troubled times

In 2011 many of Libya's people rebelled against the government of Colonel Muammar Gaddafi. The rebels took control of many Libyan cities but the government fought back, using the army and air force to attack its own people. In late 2011, Gaddafi was killed and the rebels began to form a new government. Many Libyans hoped that these dramatic events would make Libya more open to the outside world. Before the revolution, Libya had been a very isolated society.

YOUNG PEOPLE

Libya is a young country with a third of its population under the age of 15. Young people were at the heart of anti-government protests that erupted in 2011. Most young people have to do military service in Libya. Many also find it difficult to get jobs.

Libya is the fourth largest country in Africa. The shifting sands of the Sahara Desert cover much of the country.

History: crossroads of cultures

The first settlers probably came to Libya more than 10,000 years ago. Carvings and cave paintings tell us that the land was much greener than the desert landscape of today. The first people of Libya were probably **Berbers**, also called *Imazighen*. They gradually settled in small groups and became farmers. The people of ancient Egypt knew about the Libyans. In fact, kings from Libya ruled ancient Egypt from about 945 to 730 BC.

Rock carvings like this one show that wild animals and plants flourished in Libya in prehistoric times.

Phoenicians and Greeks

Around 900 to 700 BC, **Phoenicians** from the area that is now Lebanon began to trade along Africa's north coast. Trading posts were set up along the Libyan coast, including the city that would become Tripoli, Libya's modern capital. Ancient Greeks also settled the coast and set up the city of Cyrene, one of the most important centres for art and culture in the Greek world.

Roman Libya

In the first century BC, Tripolitania, the region ruled from the Phoenician city of Carthage, and Cyrenaica, the Greek **colony**, came under the rule of ancient Rome. The Romans ruled the region for centuries and built great cities such as Leptis Magna.

The arrival of Islam

One of the most significant events in Libya's history was the Arab invasion in AD 642. Muhammad, the founder of **Islam**, had died in 632 and quickly his followers spread their religion across most of North Africa.

The Roman city of Leptis Magna became one of the most beautiful cities of the **Roman Empire** during the reign of Emperor Septimius Severus (AD 193–211).

The Ottoman Empire

In the centuries following the arrival of Islam, the cities of the North African region known as the **Maghreb** (modern Libya, Tunisia, Algeria, and Morocco) were centres of learning and culture. Modern Libya is actually made up of three different regions. Tripolitania is in the northwest around Tripoli, with Cyrenaica to the east and Fezzan in the southern desert. In the 1500s, these regions became part of the Turkish **Ottoman Empire**.

Italian occupation and war

In the late 1800s, the Ottomans' power began to decline, and European countries invaded many African countries to rule them as part of their own **empires**. Italy invaded Libya in 1911. Italian rule was not popular. Nonetheless, by World War II (1939–1945), one-fifth of Libya's population was made up of settlers from Italy.

World War II changed everything. North Africa saw fierce fighting, and the Libyan city of Benghazi suffered more than 1,000 air raids as Allied forces tried to defeat German and Italian troops. After the war, the **United Nations** agreed to create a united country of Libya from the three regions of Tripolitania, Cyrenaica, and Fezzan.

Fighting in Libya during World War II destroyed many of Libya's buildings and roads.

UMAR AL-MUKHTAR (1862–1931)

Umar al-Mukhtar is revered as a Libyan national hero. He led a fierce **guerrilla** war against the Italian army in the 1920s. The Italians brutally punished anyone who sheltered the rebels. In 1931, Umar al-Mukhtar was captured and hanged in front of 20,000 people.

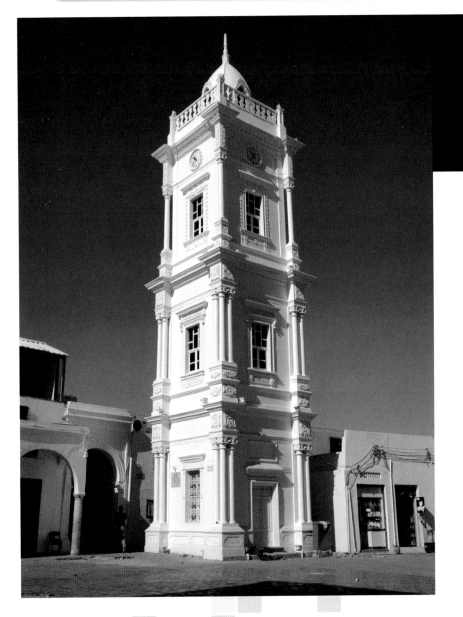

Centuries of Ottoman rule left their mark on Libya with buildings like this clock tower in Tripoli.

Independence

On 24 December 1951, King Idris I declared Libya an independent country. At first, the new Libya was friendly to **Western** countries, including the United States. With little wealth of its own, Libya relied on foreign aid.

All that changed in 1959 when oil was discovered in Libya. Libya was now able to survive on its own. Unhappy about the king's pro-Western policies, a group of army officers led by Colonel Muammar Gaddafi took power on 1 September 1969.

COLONEL MUAMMAR GADDAFI
(1942-2011)

Colonel Gaddafi was the Arab world's longest serving leader and held total power in Libya until the rebellion of 2011. Born in a tent in the desert, he came to power at the age of 27. Gaddafi argued strongly for **unity** among Arab states and unity within Africa. His support for terrorist groups brought him into conflict with Western countries. US forces bombed Libya in 1986, killing his adopted daughter. His brutal response to rebels in 2011 once again made him a villain in the eyes of many people. He was forced out of power during the Libyan civil war and killed in uncertain circumstances.

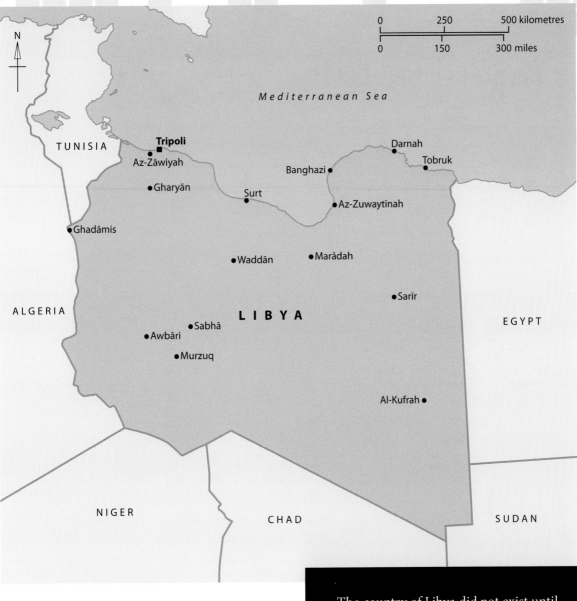

The country of Libya did not exist until after World War II. This political map shows Libya's borders and main cities.

Gaddafi's Libya

When Colonel Gaddafi came to power, Libya changed dramatically. Although Gaddafi was in power for more than 40 years, and Libya's people became wealthier than ever before, Libya's recent history has not been smooth. After an assassination attempt, Gaddafi created a large security network to reinforce his own power. This enabled Gaddafi to defeat anyone who dared to oppose his rule. However, in 2011, rebels who opposed the regime began fighting Gaddafi loyalists, and finally defeated them, after months of civil war.

Regions and resources: mineral wealth

Libya is the fourth largest country in Africa. At 1,759,540 square kilometres (679,362 square miles), it is over three times the size of France. Yet Libya has a population of just over 6 million people. This means that there is a lot of land without people.

Libya has two main regions: the coastal strip along the Mediterranean Sea and the huge, empty Sahara Desert to the south. Libya shares borders with Egypt to the east, Sudan, Chad, and Niger to the south, and Algeria and Tunisia to the west.

This physical map shows the terrain of Libya. Normally, a physical map would show rivers, but Libya doesn't have any.

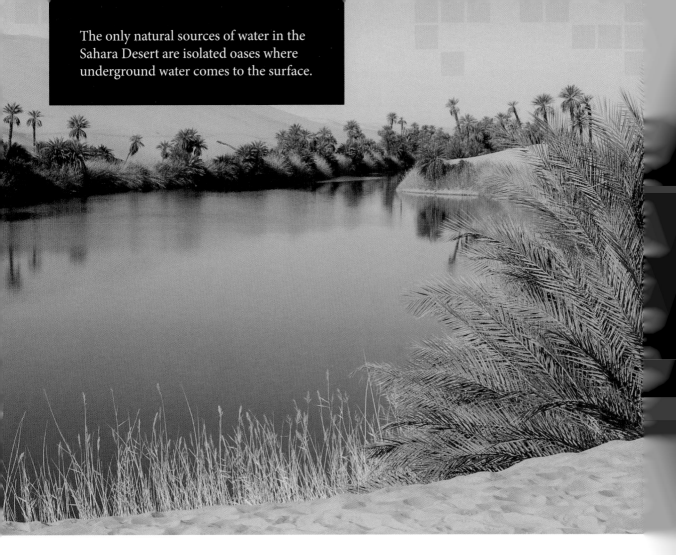

The only natural sources of water in the Sahara Desert are isolated oases where underground water comes to the surface.

Only a tiny amount of Libya's land is used for **agriculture**. This is mostly along the 1,770 kilometres (1,100 miles) of the Mediterranean coastal strip. Most people live in this area, too. The coastal plain rises up to the Nefusah **Plateau**. In the northeastern corner of Libya are the Akhdar, or green, Mountains.

Sahara Desert

Beyond these mountains, the desert takes over and covers about 90 per cent of Libya. Almost nothing grows there – much is sandy with huge dunes that move with the wind. Further south, the desert is more mountainous. Libya's tallest mountains are on the southern border with Chad.

Libya has no natural rivers. **Wadis** are dry riverbeds in the desert that fill up when it rains and then quickly run dry.

Weather and climate

Libya has a hot **climate**. Temperatures in the Sahara Desert typically reach more than 50°C (122°F). Desert temperatures fall dramatically at night because there are no clouds to keep warm air close to the ground. Deep in the desert, there is an average of less than 25 millimetres (1 inch) of rain each year. In some areas, it may not rain for several years. Near the Mediterranean coast, there is some rainfall, and temperatures are lower.

In the spring, the *ghibli* wind can raise violent dust storms in the desert regions. These can blow into the coastal strip, turn the sky red with dust, and raise the temperature 50°C for several days.

Water

With such a dry climate, lack of water is a problem. Beneath the Libyan desert are reserves of water. Some reserves have been brought to the surface and pumped to Libya's cities. Many believe this "Great Man-made River" project might eventually exhaust all Libya's water reserves and cause desert **oases** to disappear.

This chart shows the average rainfall and daily temperature for each month in Tripoli, Libya.

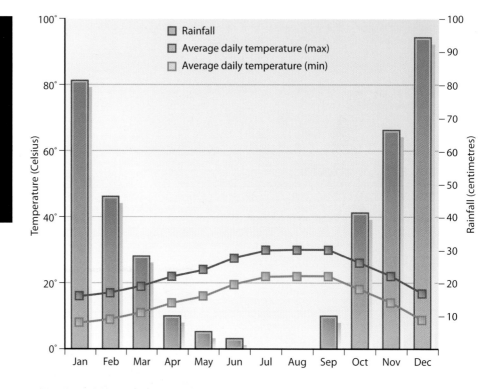

How to say...

Most people in Libya speak Arabic and so use a different alphabet from the one used in English. The following Arabic words are written as they would appear in the English alphabet:

sunny	*mushmis* (moosh-miss)	**rain**	*matir* (mah-tir)
hot	*harr* (hahrr)	**cold**	*barid* (bear-id)
storm	*asif* (a-sif)	**desert**	*sahra* (sa-ha-rah)

In a dust storm, strong winds lift tiny pieces of dust high into the air. The dust can travel hundreds of miles.

Economy

When Libya gained independence in 1951, it depended on foreign aid to keep its **economy** going. Today, Libya is the richest country in Africa. How did this happen? The answer is simple: oil.

Libya's economy is dominated by oil. Every country needs oil to run cars and aeroplanes, for example. Most countries have to **import** oil. Countries that have a lot of oil in the ground sell it to other countries and become very wealthy. Since oil was discovered in 1959, Libya has been able to build modern roads and cities with money from selling this essential **mineral**.

Libya has some of the world's largest **oil reserves** (see table on the next page). Most are located in the Sirte basin. Oil companies also believe there is more oil to be found in Libya. In addition to oil, Libya has large reserves of natural gas and smaller amounts of other minerals, such as iron and potash. Potash is used to make fertilizers that help crops grow.

This map shows the oil reserves that have been found in Libya.

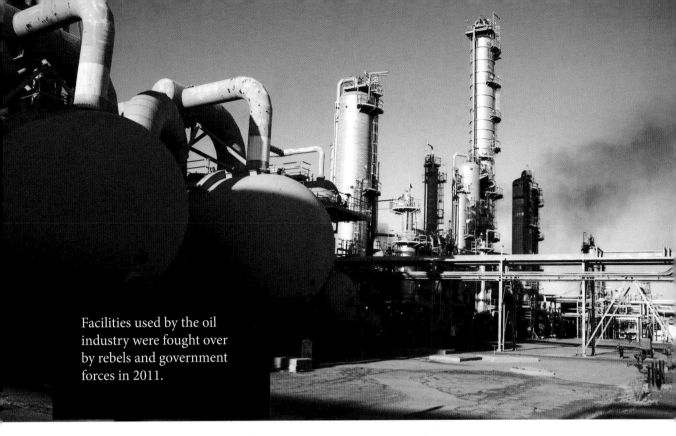

Facilities used by the oil industry were fought over by rebels and government forces in 2011.

Disadvantages

Oil has brought great wealth to Libya, but its effects have not all been positive. Libya's economy relies heavily on oil, and other industries have not really developed. If Libya's oil runs out, it would be a huge problem for the country.

Countries with the Largest Oil Reserves	Amount of Oil (in billions of barrels)
Saudi Arabia	264.6
Venezuela	172.3
Iran	137.6
Iraq	115.0
Kuwait	101.5
United Arab Emirates	97.8
Russian Federation	74.2
Libya	44.3
Kazakhstan	39.8
Nigeria	37.2

Source: BP Statistical Review of World Energy 2010

Other industries

Apart from industry related to oil, such as making oil drums, there is little industry in Libya. The **petrochemical** industry is also linked to oil. Products taken from oil are used to make everyday things – from plastic containers to cleaning fluids.

Food and farming

Before the discovery of oil, most of Libya's people farmed the land. However, Libya has never been well-suited to growing crops, and only 1 per cent of Libya's land is used to grow food. Wheat, vegetables, olives, and some citrus fruits (such as oranges and lemons) are grown in a couple of regions.

Outside where crops are grown, **scrubland** has just enough **vegetation** for animals, such as goats and sheep, to feed. Elsewhere in the country, apart from around desert oases, there is not enough water to grow crops. Many foods are imported, and ambitious **irrigation** projects such as the "Great Man-made River" increase the area in Libya that can be farmed.

Daily life

Although oil has brought wealth, it has not always brought jobs for the many people who have moved to Libya's cities. Around one in three people of working age in Libya do not have a job. This **unemployment** problem affects young people in particular. When people do not have a job and cannot earn any money, they become unhappy. Libyans blamed the government for not providing enough jobs. High unemployment was one cause of protests against the government that led to the Libyan rebellion of 2011.

Migrant workers

Many workers move to Libya from elsewhere in Africa. Some stay in Libya and work in industry and farming. Others plan to save enough money to travel across the Mediterranean Sea to European countries, such as Italy and Malta.

Oil is plentiful in Libya, but water is a scarce and precious resource. This circle of crops in the desert is irrigated by water from deep underground.

Wildlife: surviving in the desert

Animals and plants need water to live, and the Sahara Desert is a difficult place for most animals to survive. According to ancient rock carvings, thousands of years ago lions, elephants, and giraffes were found in this region. But as the desert became drier and hotter, these animals were forced to move further south.

Blending in

Large animals that are able to survive in Libya include gazelle and *waddan*. The *waddan* is also called the Barbary sheep, although it is more closely related to the goat. This sure-footed animal lives in rocky, dry areas and has adapted to its **habitat**. It can survive without water for long periods. When threatened, the *waddan* stands completely still. Its sandy red colour helps it to blend in with the surroundings. In the areas where the *waddan* lives, there is no **vegetation** to hide behind.

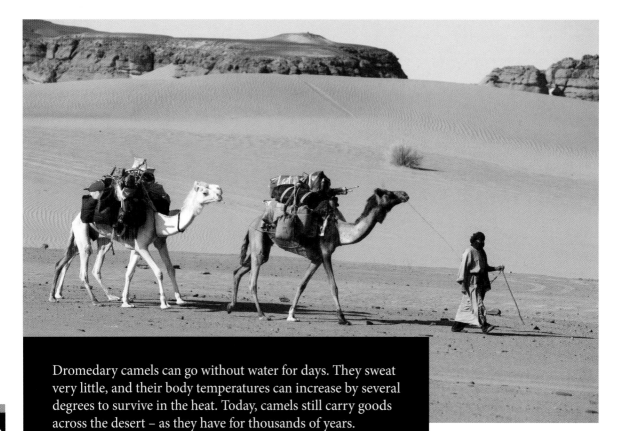

Dromedary camels can go without water for days. They sweat very little, and their body temperatures can increase by several degrees to survive in the heat. Today, camels still carry goods across the desert – as they have for thousands of years.

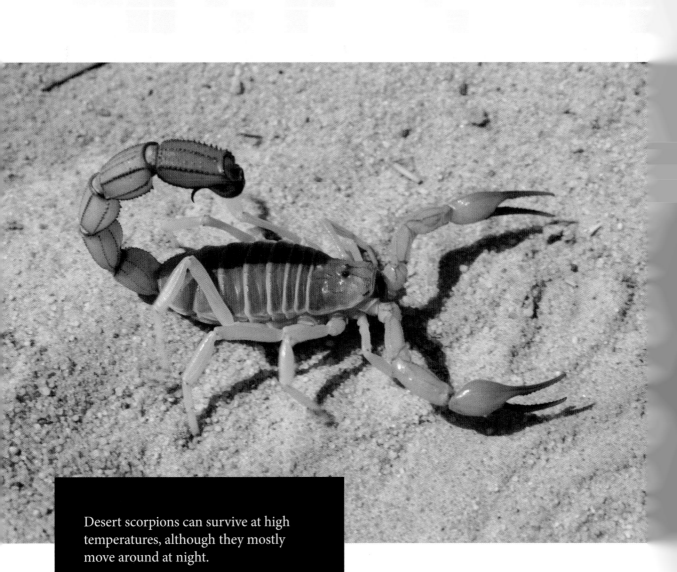

Desert scorpions can survive at high temperatures, although they mostly move around at night.

Many non-mammals can survive in the desert. Reptiles, such as snakes and lizards, are **cold-blooded** creatures that rely on the heat of the sun to keep them alive. Even so, many, like the Sahara sand viper, bury themselves in the sand to protect themselves from the heat. They lie in wait for small mammals they might eat.

Plant life

Libya's coastal strip is rich in vegetation, including herbs, such as the asphodel. The only area of natural forest in Libya is on the northern edge of the Akhdar Mountains where cypress, juniper, and Aleppo pine trees face the sea and are sheltered from the heat of the desert.

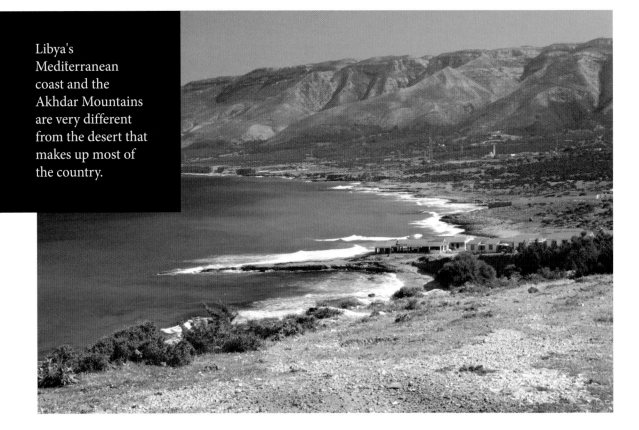

Libya's Mediterranean coast and the Akhdar Mountains are very different from the desert that makes up most of the country.

How to say...

camel	*jamal* (ja-mahl)	horse	*hisan* (hi-sahn)
sheep	*kharuuf* (ka-roof)	tree	*shajara* (sha-ja-rah)
water	*ma'* (maya)	flower	*zahra* (zah-ra)

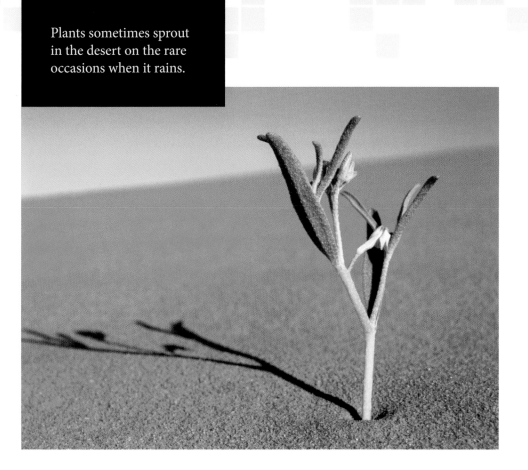

Plants sometimes sprout in the desert on the rare occasions when it rains.

Away from the sea, some grasses grow in the areas of **scrubland**. Out in the desert, there is almost no vegetation. Only acacia trees provide shelter from the sun. These trees have very small leaves and long roots to capture any water they can. When occasional rains come to the desert, grasses will suddenly sprout up close to the **wadis**, dry ravines that briefly fill with water.

Desertification

The Sahara Desert is the world's biggest desert. It is about the size of the United States, and it continues to expand. Temperatures around the world are rising. This means that more places around the edges of deserts are becoming too hot and dry for plants to grow. Using underground water sources to **irrigate** crops adds to the problem. This **desertification** could affect Libya in two ways. First, it may mean that areas in Libya become even drier than they are now so that it is even more difficult to grow food. Second, people might move to countries such as Libya from south of the Sahara due to the growing desert.

Infrastructure: dictatorship to revolution

In 1977 Gaddafi wrote *The Green Book*, which set out Libya's political system. Gaddafi was officially called the Leader of the Revolution. For more than 40 years, he held almost total power in the country but in 2011 people across North Africa demanded change (see table).

Country	Political Change
Algeria	Widespread protests erupted against the government and rising food prices in 2011. President Abdelaziz Bouteflika promised to introduce **reforms**.
Egypt	President Hosni Mubarak resigned on February 11, 2011, after 30 years in power. A military government took over until new elections could be held.
Libya	In February 2011, many Libyans protested at the rule of Muammar Gaddafi, who responded by attacking his opponents with tanks and aircraft. The **United Nations** agreed to military action to protect Libya's people. Gaddafi was killed in October 2011.
Morocco	King Muhammad VI announced economic and political reforms following huge demonstrations in February 2011. The king controls many aspects of politics in Morocco.
Tunisia	President Zine al-Abidine Ben Ali stepped down in January 2011 following huge protests against his government. The new government has introduced democratic and legal reforms.

Mustafa Abdul Jalil, shown here, is the leader of the National Transitional Council of Libya. The Council represents the anti-Gaddafi rebels. The Council took over power in Libya in September 2011.

Under Gaddafi, Libya's people did not vote directly for the government as they would in a **democracy** like the United Kingdom. Each community had a local representative in the Libyan **parliament**, called the General People's **Congress**. The General People's Congress elected a committee to run the country, but important decisions were taken by Colonel Gaddafi.

The battle for Libya

In 2011 rebels took control of parts of Libya, particularly in the east around Benghazi. The rebels planned to "guide the country to free elections and the establishment of a constitution" once Gaddafi had been forced from power. The rebels finally defeated Gaddafi's forces and the dictator was killed. The National Transitional Council now has control of the country and hopes to stabilize the government.

Religion and the law

Religion is an important part of Libyan life. The country's laws are based on **Islamic**, or **sharia**, principles. They follow rules laid down in the Koran, the **Muslim** holy book

Living in Libya

The money Libya has made from oil has helped the Libyan people in many ways. Free healthcare and benefits, including pensions for the elderly, are provided – this is unusual for an African country. Education is also free for all Libyans.

Going to school

All Libyans have to go to school from the ages of 6 to 15. Children attend elementary school for six years and middle and high school for three years each. About 80 per cent of Libyans can read and write. Although girls and boys have equal treatment in the Libyan school system, families often do not send girls to school for very long. University education is also free for Libyans.

Sanctions

In the 1990s, Libya's people were negatively affected by trade **sanctions**. Other countries were banned from trading with Libya because of Libya's support of **terrorists**. After the sanctions ended in 2003, the government tried to improve Libya's **economy** but change was difficult because of the government's tight control of many parts of Libyan life and industry.

Rights and freedoms

Since 2003, Libya's government and people have been much more open to influence from other countries. Colonel Gaddafi's government, however, still controlled many aspects of life. Libyans did not enjoy many of the rights that people enjoy in most democratic countries.

When Libyans protested against the government in February 2011, they were arrested and attacked by Gaddafi's forces. Now the National Transitional Council is working to ensure the safety and liberation of all citizens.

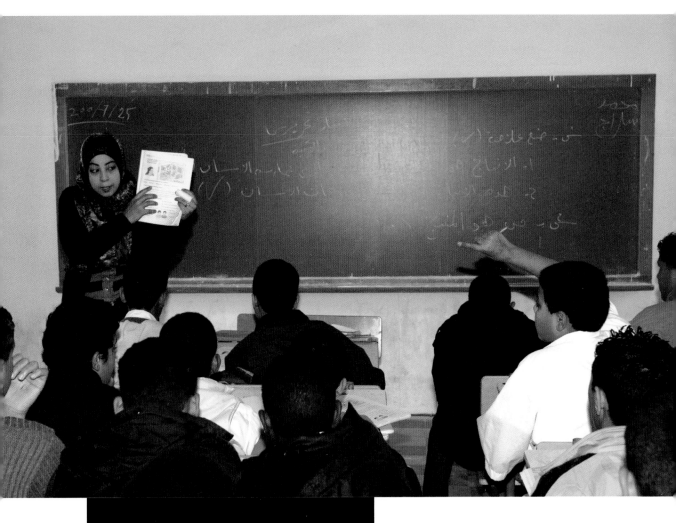

Arabic is the primary language in school. Young people also learn English and have religious instruction.

Culture: tradition and Islam

The **Berbers** settled in Libya thousands of years ago. Over the centuries, this group mixed with Arabs who invaded or settled in Libya. Most of the people in Libya today have a mix of Berber and Arab ancestry. They speak Arabic as well as Berber languages. **Islam** is Libya's main religion and has an enormous influence on many parts of daily life in Libya.

Most Libyan people now live in cities. Tripoli is the largest city. The desert in Libya's south has very few people. Some *Tuareg* people still live in the desert areas. These **nomadic** people traditionally travel across the desert. Many *Tuareg* today are now settling in one location.

Tuareg men traditionally wear a veil in public. Tuareg women generally do not wear veils.

Home and family life

Families are very important in Libya. People often live in large family groups that include parents, their unmarried children, and married sons with their own families. There are strict traditions surrounding family life. Although men and women have equal rights in Libya, they traditionally have very different roles. Most married women do not work outside the home.

Daily life

Family homes are very private places in Libya. They have no outside windows at ground level, and guests are only invited to certain parts of the house. Inside the walls of the house, there may be beautiful gardens where the family can keep cool away from the heat of the bustling city.

In Libya, several generations of a family will often live together.

Religion and the arts

Religion is at the centre of Libyan life. The month of **Ramadan** is a key event in the Libyan calendar. During the month, **Muslims** fast, or do not eat, between sunrise and sunset. The festival of *Eid-ul-Fitr* at the end of Ramadan is a huge celebration.

Most Islamic art does not show images of people or animals, and this is also true of Libyan art. Folk arts include weaving, embroidery, and metalwork. The works featuring beautiful patterns and designs are often displayed in **mosques**, such as the Karamanli and Gurgi mosques in Tripoli.

Libya has many successful writers, but few are known outside the Arabic-speaking world. Much of Libyan writing has been concerned with politics. Under the Gaddafi regime, writers were not allowed to be critical, so much of the writing favoured the government.

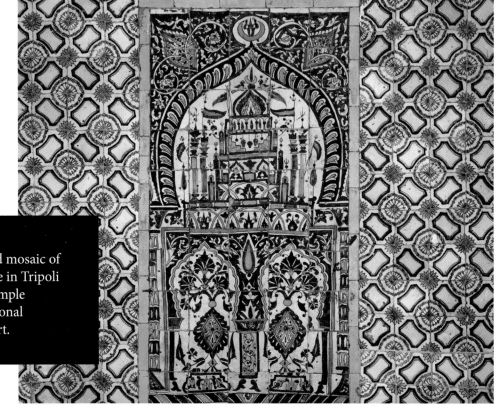

This tiled mosaic of a mosque in Tripoli is an example of traditional Libyan art.

Music and dance

Music is an important part of celebrations. Traditional music and folk dancing go together. Libyan music is played on instruments such as the *gheeta*, similar to a clarinet, and the *zukra* pipes. *Malouf* is often performed at weddings and involves a large group of musicians who sing and recite poetry about love or religion.

Folk dancing is common at Libyan festivals

Although there is a Libyan music industry, most pop music comes from Egypt, Tunisia, and Algeria.

IBRAHIM AL-KOUNI (B.1948)

Novelist Ibrahim al-Kouni's work is known across the Arab world and has been translated into many languages. Al-Kouni was born in the Libyan desert. His writing reflects his fascination with the Sahara Desert.

Food and shopping

Libyan food is much like the cuisine from the rest of North Africa. **Couscous** is part of many meals. Italian food has also had an influence. Pasta is the main ingredient in some dishes.

Family meals

Family meals are very important to Libyans. The family usually eats together unless there are guests. When guests are invited, men and women often eat separately. Before the main meal of the day, the family sits together, and water is passed around for hand washing. Everyone eats from a shared bowl, using only the right hand. In Libya, it is rude to use the left hand.

Libyan meals often have many courses, including spiced soups, salads, and main courses that mix meat with couscous or rice. In the cities, people buy food at the local *souq*, or market. Many Libyans also love sweets and pastries. Many small shops sell them. A traditional Libyan tea is often the last course of the meal.

Horse racing is a popular sport that often takes place on special days and holidays.

YOUNG PEOPLE

Football is the most popular sport in Libya. Tripoli and Benghazi are home to many of the top Libyan football teams. Young Libyans also follow Italian football. In fact, one of Colonel Gaddafi's sons briefly played for an Italian team. The African Cup of Nations is scheduled to be played in Libya in 2013.

Celebrations

Food is at the heart of many Libyan celebrations, such as weddings, which often last for several days.

Shaba Libiya (Libyan Soup)

Different variations of this soup are served at the beginning of many meals in Libya. Ask an adult to help you make it.

Ingredients

- 450 g chopped stewing lamb
- 1 can chickpeas
- 1 chopped onion
- 2-3 tablespoons of tomato puree
- 1 tablespoon of dried mint or handful of parsley leaves
- ½ teaspoon each of ground coriander, tumeric, and chilli powder
- 3 tablespoons of olive oil
- About 1 litre of water

What to do

1. Heat the oil and fry the onion until soft. Add the lamb, chickpeas, tomato puree and spices.
2. Cover the mixture with water and simmer for 35-40 minutes until the lamb is cooked.
3. Before serving, stir in dried mint or parsley.

Libya today

Libya has seen many changes since the discovery of oil in 1959. Before oil was discovered, most Libyans lived outside cities. Today, those cities are home to about 80 per cent of Libyans. Despite huge political and economic changes, Libyans have kept many traditional parts of their way of life, based around **Islam** and family.

For many years, Libyans had little contact with other countries. The government's support for **terrorists** meant the country had few friends around the world. This was starting to change until Colonel Gaddafi's attacks on Libya's people after the protests in early 2011. People around the world condemned the Libyan leader and warplanes from many countries attacked Gaddafi's forces to protect the people of Libya.

Protesters wave Libya's flag in Benghazi on 11 April 2011.

How to say...

Hello	*marhaban* (marr-hab-an)
Goodbye	*ila al'likaa* (il-al-likaac)
Yes	*na'am* (nahm)
No	*la'a* (le-ah)
How are you?	*kaifa haluka?* (kay-fa ha-look)
My name is ...	*ana ismee ...* (an-a is-mee)

The future

Libya's future is uncertain. Its new government faces many challenges. Libya's cities and oil industry have been badly damaged by the conflict. Many Libyans have also been forced to leave their country. After 40 years of being governed by Muammar Gaddafi, how will Libya adjust to a future without him?

Oil is vital to Libya's **economy** but our use of oil and other fossil fuels is causing climate change that could be particularly damaging to countries with a hot climate, such as Libya.

Fact file

Country Name:	Libyan Republic
Capital:	Tripoli (population: 2,189,000)
Language:	Arabic, but Italian and English also spoken
Religion:	Islam (97%), Other (2%)
Government:	National Transitional Council overseeing move to democracy
National anthem:	"Allahu Akbar" ("God is Greatest")

God is Greatest!
God is Greatest!
He is above the plots of the aggressors,
And He is the best helper of the oppressed.
With faith and with weapons I shall defend my country,
And the light of truth will shine in my hand.
Sing with me!
Sing with me!
God is Greatest!
God is Greatest!
God, God, God is Greatest!
God is above the aggressors.

Population:	6,461,454 (est. 2010)
Life Expectancy:	77.7 years (75.3 years for men, 80.1 years for women)
Bordering Countries:	Egypt, Sudan, Chad, Niger, Algeria, and Tunisia
Total Land Area:	1,759,540 square kilometres (679,362 square miles)
Largest Cities:	Benghazi, Al Hums, Az Zawiyah, Misratah, Zuwarah

Coastline:	1,770 kilometres (1,100 miles) along the Mediterranean Sea
Highest Elevation:	Bikku Bitti, 2,267 metres (7,438 feet) along border with Chad
Major Rivers:	No permanent rivers
Oil Reserves:	44.3 billion barrels
Other Natural Resources:	natural gas, gypsum
Currency:	Libyan Dinar = 1,000 dirhams
Unemployment Rate:	30%
Roads:	100,024 kilometres (62,152 miles); 57,214 kilometres (35,551 miles) paved

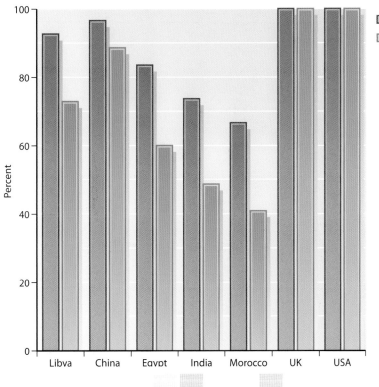

Literacy rate (male)
Literacy rate (female)

Percent

Libya   China   Egypt   India   Morocco   UK   USA

This chart compares the proportion of people who can read and write in Libya and other countries.

Famous Libyans: Ali Omar Ermes (b.1945), artist

Ahmed Fakroun (b.1953), musician

Mustafa Muhammad Abdul Jalil (b.1952), former Minister of Justice and leader of Libyan rebels' National Council

Ibrahim al-Kuoni (b.1948), author

Colonel Muammar Gaddafi (1942–2011), Libyan leader 1969 to 2011

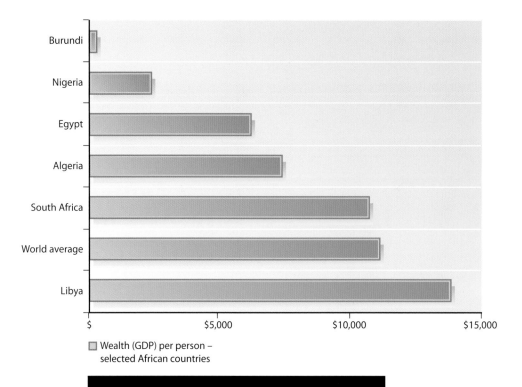

Wealth (GDP) per person – selected African countries

The value of everything produced in a country is called the Gross Domestic Product (GDP). Libya's GDP per person is higher than in other African countries, mainly because the country makes lots of money from oil.

Libya's UNESCO World Heritage sites

World heritage sites must be outstanding examples of historical or natural interest. Libya's five world heritage sites highlight different parts of the country's history.

- **Cyrene**: centre of ancient Greek civilization in Libya

- **Leptis Magna**: amazing ruins of a beautiful Roman city

- **Sabratha**: ruins of Phoenician trading post

- **Tadrart Acacus**: cave paintings that show the way of life in the Sahara up to 12,000 years ago

- **Old city of Ghadamès** (pictured below): example of an ancient Saharan city with traditional buildings

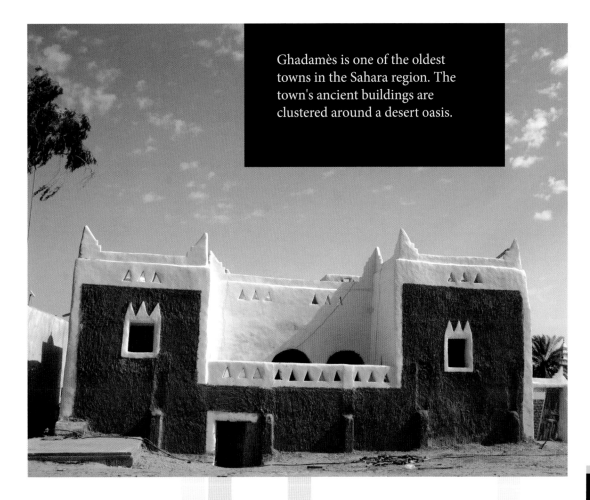

Ghadamès is one of the oldest towns in the Sahara region. The town's ancient buildings are clustered around a desert oasis.

Timeline

BC is short for "before Christ". BC is added after a date and means that the date occurred before the birth of Jesus Christ, for example, 450 BC.

AD is short for Anno Domini, which is Latin for "in the year of our Lord". AD is added before a date and means that the date occurred after the birth of Jesus Christ, for example, AD 720.

BC

c. 8000　Earliest evidence of settlements in Libya.

c. 1000　**Phoenician** traders establish trading posts on the Libyan coast.

63　Ancient Greek settlers found the city of Cyrene.

46　Julius Caesar adds Tripolitania to the Roman province of Africa; Cyrenaica and Tripolitania united in the first century AD.

AD

193　Septimus Severus becomes Roman emperor; Libyan city of Leptis Magna rebuilt and expanded.

642　Arab invaders begin to arrive in Libya, bringing **Islamic** faith.

1551　**Ottoman Empire** occupies Tripoli.

1911　Italy occupies Libya.

1942　Allied forces push Italians out of Libya, which is then divided into British and French regions.

1951　Libya declares its independence on 24 December; King Idris becomes head of state.

1959　Oil first discovered in Libya.

1969　Military government led by Colonel Muammar Gaddafi takes over from the King of Libya on 1 September.

1973	Gaddafi launches a "cultural revolution" creating people's committees in many workplaces and areas of society.
1975-1979	Gaddafi publishes three volumes of the *Green Book*, which sets out his ideas for the government of Libya.
1986	US forces bomb Tripoli and Benghazi on 15 April.
1988	On 21 December, Pan Am flight 103 explodes over Lockerbie, Scotland, killing 270 people; Libyan man later convicted of causing the explosion.
1992	United Nations imposes sanctions on Libya, affecting Libya's trade and relations with other countries.
2003	United Nations sanctions lifted and Gaddafi promises to end development of chemical and biological weapons and stop support of terrorists.
2005	Gaddafi announces steps to modernize Libyan **economy**.
2009	Gaddafi becomes leader of the African Union; he calls for a "United States of Africa".
2010	European Union and Libya sign agreement on immigration.
2011	In February government troops fire on a protest in Benghazi following the arrest of a human rights activist. Protests spread across the country. A transitional government forms and an army of rebels fight Gaddafi's loyalists. Gaddafi is forced to leave power and go into hiding. The National Transitional Council takes over Libya's government. Gaddafi is killed in October 2011.

Glossary

agriculture farming; the production of crops or livestock

Berbers people, also called *Imazighen*, who lived in North Africa before the arrival, in the AD 600s, of Arab settlers from the east

climate general weather conditions over a long time, including temperature and precipitation, such as rain or snow

cold-blooded having a body temperature that changes with the environment

colony area controlled by a foreign country. Usually, people from the foreign country live in the area.

congress group of officials or representatives that meet to discuss issues

couscous cracked wheat, originally from North Africa, that is served with meat and vegetables

democracy form of government by the people or by the elected representatives of the people

desertification the process of fertile land becoming desert

dictatorship government by a ruler, or dictator, with total power who often takes power by force

economy management of the resources, finances, income, and expenses of a community or country

empire political unit that controls a very large area, usually broken into several separate countries or territories

guerrilla any armed group that is not part of a regular army, usually fighting against a larger force or invading army

habitat natural environment for a living being

import ship goods into a country from other nations

irrigate supply water to fields and land to grow crops

Islam religious faith of Muslims, based on the text of the Koran and teachings of the prophet Muhammad

Maghreb region of North Africa that includes Libya, Tunisia, Algeria, and Morocco

mineral substance that occurs naturally, including metals and oil

monarchy government by a king or queen

mosque place of worship for Muslims

Muslim follower of Islam, or having to do with a follower of Islam

nomadic people who do not live in one place but move according to the season or to find grazing land for animals

oasis (pl. oases) fertile area in the desert where underground water comes to the surface

oil reserves oil that has been discovered underground but not yet brought to the surface

Ottoman Empire large empire based in the city of Constantinople (now Istanbul) that ruled much of the Middle East and North Africa from the 1200s to the 1900s

parliament group of people that makes and approves the laws of a country. In a democracy, the people elect the members of parliament.

petrochemical substances made by refining and processing petroleum or natural gas

Phoenicians ancient people from present-day Lebanon and southern Syria, who traded along the coasts of the Mediterranean Sea

plateau level area of land raised above the land around it

Ramadan month of fasting, from sunrise to sunset, during the Muslim year

reform change designed to improve something

republic form of government in which the people elect their leaders

Roman Empire ruling power over much of Europe and Africa lasting from approximately 44 BC to AD 476

sanctions punishment of one country by another country or organization, usually stopping them from trading with other nations

scrubland land that has only very small plants, such as small shrubs

sharia laws based on the Koran that describe duties and penalties for Muslims

terrorist anyone who seeks to achieve political goals through violence

unemployment number or proportion of unemployed people

United Nations worldwide organization that promotes world peace and social justice

unity agreement among people or groups

vegetation plants and trees

wadi dry desert ravine that only becomes a river temporarily when it rains

Western referring to developed countries, especially in North America and Europe, but also including countries such as Australia

Find out more

Books

Deserts (Geography Fact Files), Katie Powell (Ed.) (Wayland, 2007)

Muammar Al-Qaddafi's Libya (Dictatorships), Kimberley Sullivan (Lerner, 2009)

The Middle East and North Africa (Regions of the World). Neil Morris (Heinemann Library, 2008)

The Story Behind Oil, Heidi Moore (Heinemann Library, 2009)

The Story of Islam (Usborne Young Reading: Series Three), Rob Lloyd Jones (E.D.C. Publishing, 2007)

Websites

news.bbc.co.uk/1/hi/world/africa/1398437.stm
This timeline of Libya's history on the BBC Website is updated with recent news about the country and links to news stories.

worldmusic.nationalgeographic.com/view/page.basic/region/content. region/africa_1/en_US
Learn more about the origins of the music of North Africa on this National Geographic website.

www.historyforkids.org/learn/islam/religion/
Information on the history of Islam. This site also has other sections, including African history.

Further research

Most people will not be lucky enough to visit Libya for themselves, especially as political turmoil continues to plague the country. However, you can find out more about this fascinating country by researching the topics listed below. Visit your local library or have an adult help you research the Internet for more information.

- North Africa and the Maghreb: the countries of North Africa share much of their history and culture. Find out more about Tunisia, Algeria, Morocco, and Egypt to discover the similarities and differences between Libya and these countries.

- Oil plays a very important part in Libya's story. You can find out more about where oil comes from and why it is so important.

- Libya's relations with other countries, particularly the United States and Europe, have not been easy in recent years. You can find out more about why this is. Although Libya has opened itself up to the outside world in recent years, this could still change in future.

Topic tools

You can use these topic tools for your school projects. Trace the map on to a sheet of paper, using the thick black outline to guide you.

This served as Libya's flag until 1977, when Gaddafi introduced his own flag. The National Transitional Council reintroduced this as Libya's flag in February 2011. The three stripes each represent one of Libya's three major regions: red for Fezzan; black for Cyrenaica; and green for Tripolitania. The white crescent moon and star represent Islam, Libya's main religion.

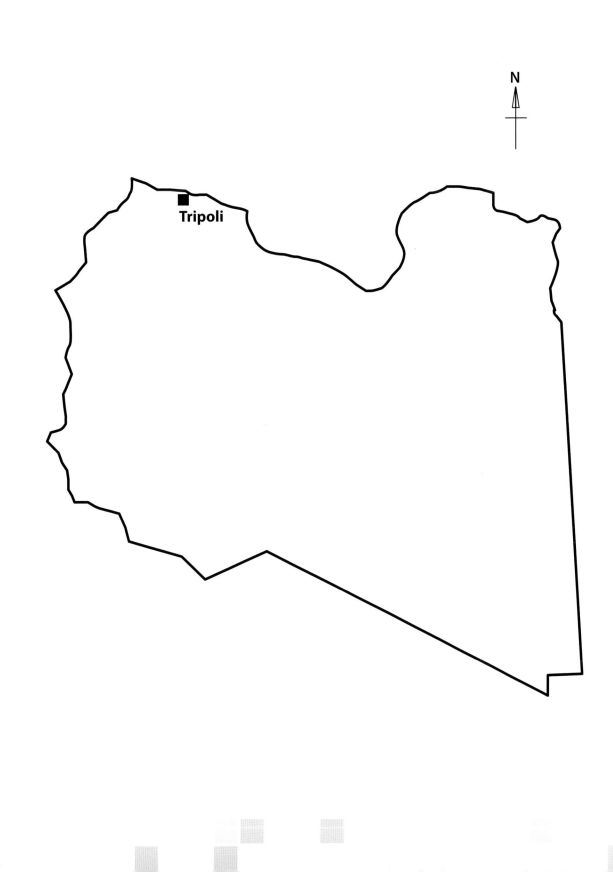

Tripoli

N

Index

Titles in the series

Afghanistan	978 1 406 22778 9	Japan	978 1 406 23548 7
Algeria	978 1 406 23561 6	Latvia	978 1 406 22795 6
Australia	978 1 406 23533 3	Liberia	978 1 406 23563 0
Brazil	978 1 406 22785 7	Libya	978 1 406 23564 7
Canada	978 1 406 23534 0	Lithuania	978 1 406 22796 3
Chile	978 1 406 22786 4	Mexico	978 1 406 22790 1
China	978 1 406 23547 0	Morocco	978 1 406 23565 4
Costa Rica	978 1 406 22787 1	New Zealand	978 1 406 23536 4
Cuba	978 1 406 22788 8	North Korea	978 1 406 23549 4
Czech Republic	978 1 406 22792 5	Pakistan	978 1 406 22782 6
Egypt	978 1 406 23562 3	Philippines	978 1 406 23550 0
England	978 1 406 22799 4	Poland	978 1 406 22797 0
Estonia	978 1 406 22793 2	Portugal	978 1 406 23578 4
France	978 1 406 22800 7	Russia	978 1 406 23579 1
Germany	978 1 406 22801 4	Scotland	978 1 406 22803 8
Greece	978 1 406 23575 3	South Africa	978 1 406 23537 1
Haiti	978 1 406 22789 5	South Korea	978 1 406 23551 7
Hungary	978 1 406 22794 9	Spain	978 1 406 23580 7
Iceland	978 1 406 23576 0	Tunisia	978 1 406 23566 1
India	978 1 406 22779 6	United States of America	978 1 406 23538 8
Iran	978 1 406 22780 2	Vietnam	978 1 406 23552 4
Iraq	978 1 406 22781 9	Wales	978 1 406 22804 5
Ireland	978 1 406 23577 7	Yemen	978 1 406 22783 3
Israel	978 1 406 23535 7		
Italy	978 1 406 22802 1		